The
TOTAL
PACKAGE

A NEW CREATURE

Nichol Collins

The Total Package A New Creature

ISBN 978-0-9997545-7-3

Online store Covenant Gear @ Globeshakers.com

The Rainbow Belongs to God Movement

Table of Contents

Fresh Path

"The acts of the flesh are obvious: sexual immorality, impurity, debauchery (sensuality), idolatry and witchcraft; hatred, discord, jealousy, fits of rage, selfish ambition, dissensions, factions, and envy; drunkenness, orgies and such like. I warn you , as I did before, that those who live like this will not inherit the Kingdom of God. Galatians 5:19-21 NIV

The flesh is superficially satisfied through sin. Once you get tired of an unfruitful lifestyle, it will provoke a change. Your soul is on a spiritual quest longing for fulfillment. The love that God has for humanity is inexhaustible. If anyone goes to hell, they actually sent themselves there. Regardless of your past, God still chooses to forgive you when you obey the Plan of Salvation. Sometimes you have to be *off* with people, to be *on* with God. In other words, some disconnections release blessings which were delayed because of being distracted by others.

"Transformed," is defined as a thorough or dramatic transition in the form, appearance, or character of. Jesus Christ turns lives completely around by the regeneration of the Holy Spirit. If biblical truths remain hidden, your endeavors will remain unsuccessful. *"Search the scriptures, for in them you think you have eternal life,"* (John 5:39). You can be <u>sincerely incorrect</u>, which is why God wants to make sure you discover the full TRUTH.

In order to effectively *overcome bondage's,* you must adhere to the word of God. You cannot ignore God's word, and allow people to persuade you with their own philosophy. The Lord loves you so much and he does not want anyone to walk in error. If you take the time to read the scriptures provided in this chapter, you will have clarity and insight.

Jesus said, *"No man can come to me, except the Father which hath sent me draw him "* (John 6:44). When an individual desires to escape from darkness, their heart is tender toward Christ. Repentance is being genuinely sorry and forsaking a lifestyle of sin. There must be a sincere desire to completely change.

The Bible NEVER said that baptism was an outward expression of an inward work, or a symbolic ritual. Baptism is actually a command. Repentance depicts Jesus' death, baptism represents his burial, and the infilling of the Holy Spirit signifies the resurrection of Christ. The 3 step plan of salvation is a type and shadow of the blood required to be smeared in 3 places on the doorpost in Exodus 12:7 to keep the death angel away from their home.

Faith comes by hearing and hearing by the word, so read aloud John 3:1-7. *Jesus answered, "Verily, verily, I say unto thee, **Except** a man be born of **water** and of the **Spirit**, he **cannot** enter into the kingdom of God."* John 3:5 (Key Verse)

Observe how Jesus emphasizes *verily, verily,* meaning truly or certainly. Also, Jesus says "verily" twice because he is trying to get your attention. He refers to being born of the flesh (a natural birth), and born of the Spirit (a spiritual birth). In John 3:7, Jesus warns us not to be surprised, but just do it! Verse 8 gives the analogy of the wind blowing but it is unidentifiable of which direction it is travelling and when the Spirit comes a sound is present.

Why would Jesus say in John 3:5 we CANNOT enter into heaven unless we are *Born Again* of the *"water and of the Spirit?"* If a person believes they are already saved without baptism or speaking in tongues, the command in John 3:5 should provoke one to obey the scriptures, and receive the fullness of God's inheritance.

*"He that **believeth** and is **baptized** shall be saved: but he that believeth not shall be damned. And these signs shall follow them that believe; In my name shall they cast out devils; they shall **speak with new tongues**."* Mark 16:16-17 (water & Spirit)

Jesus mentioned baptism and the Holy Spirit in John 3:5 and Mark 16:16-17. Also, the *"keys of the kingdom of heaven"* were given to Peter in Matthew 16:19 and are only mentioned *once* in the Bible. Jesus delegated him with the badge of authority. On the Day of Pentecost, Apostle Peter used those spiritual keys to open the door proclaiming the Plan of Salvation in Acts 2:38.

For another reference point, read Acts 1:3-9. It states that Jesus spent 40 days after His resurrection giving instructions to his disciples (followers). He also mentioned John "baptized" with water but the Holy Spirit would be poured out in a few days. The last words Jesus spoke before ascending back into heaven was a command to wait for the promise. Once again, the water and Spirit is reiterated.

*"But ye shall receive power **after** that the Holy Ghost is come upon you: and you shall be my witnesses."* Acts 1:8

You cannot live holy without the Holy Spirit.

We have no power until *after* receiving the infilling of the Holy Spirit. Satan tries to convince believers that it's unnecessary to speak in tongues. A spiritual battle cannot be won without being fully equipped.

Let's summarize this chain of events in Acts chapter two. Read Acts 2:1-4 and notice, they ALL were filled and spoke in other *"tongues."* Browse down to Acts 2:13-17 and see how critics began to accuse them of being drunk on new wine. Peter stood up to address the crowd because he was delegated with the authority by Jesus in Matthew 16:19 (Keys of the Kingdom). Peter declared in Acts 2:17 that this out pour of the Holy Spirit is a fulfillment, of what was foretold by Joel. God said, "I am pouring out my Spirit upon ALL flesh in the last days" (Joel 2:28, Acts 2:17). Peter proceeded to preach a sermon. He began to remind the onlookers of all the miracles they witnessed Jesus perform (Acts 2:22), but yet they murdered him anyway. Peter testified that those with him were also witnesses that Jesus had risen from the dead (Acts 2:32).

PLAN OF SALVATION

*"Now when they heard this, they were pricked in their heart, and said unto Peter and to the rest of the apostles, Men and brethren, what shall we do?" Then Peter said unto them, " **Repent**, and **be baptized every one** of you in the **name of Jesus Christ** for the remission of sins, and ye shall **receive** the **gift** of the **Holy Ghost**. For the **promise** is unto you, and to your children, and to all that are afar off, even as many as the Lord our God shall call. And with many other words did he testify and exhort, saying, **Save yourselves** from this untoward generation."* Acts 2:37-40

There is not a period [.] after the word "repent" in Acts 2:38, a comma means there is a continuation following. The remainder of the verse states that **everyone** should be *baptized* in the name of *Jesus Christ* and you will receive the *gift of the Holy Spirit*. When baking a cake, all of the ingredients must be added. In the same aspect, we cannot leave out steps of salvation and assume that we are saved. The Lord honors one who is genuinely seeking Him, and will be faithful to direct your path. It is our choice to humbly obey the word of God. What will it hurt?

Repentance is a preparation to be baptized.

Water baptism is a cleansing process, that requires faith in the shed blood of Jesus which grants us forgiveness and remission of sins. Peter also tells us that *baptism also <u>saves us</u> and is an answer of a good conscience toward God* (1 Peter 3:20-21). The primary purpose of baptism represents your faith in a crucified, buried, and risen Savior. Baptism is an act of obedience, and a transliteration of the Greek word Baptizo, which means to "immerse."

*"And whatsoever ye do in word or deed, do **all** in the name of the Lord **Jesus**, giving thanks to God and the Father by him."* Colossians 3:17

We as human beings are comprised of a body, soul, and spirit; yet we are ONE person identified by <u>our name</u>. There is NO baptism in the entire Bible performed in the titles/nouns of the Father, Son, and Holy Spirit. The Britannica, Canney, and Hastings encyclopedia have recorded that the early church always baptized in the name of the Lord Jesus until development of the Trinity doctrine in the 2nd century by Roman Catholics. The word trinity initially originated from Plato which was defined as black magic, geometry, and religion. Trinity was plagiarized by the Catholic church and redefined as the Father, Son, and Holy Ghost. They started sprinkling babies and adults instead of immersion.

A criminal's record is not erased unless it has been expunged. Our sins are eradicated when we are buried in the liquid grave of baptism. Even a bride takes on the last name of the groom, so as Believer's we are God's bride which is befitting to take on our Savior's name (JESUS). Being baptized in the name of JESUS is the right way because it aligns with examples in scripture. If the titles of the Father, Son, and Holy Spirit were recited during your baptism ceremony as the formula; you definitely need to be **re-baptized** in the name of **Jesus Christ.** I plead with you to humbly submit.

"Don't you know that all of us who were baptized into Christ Jesus were baptized into His death? We were therefore buried with Him through baptism into death in order that, just as Christ was raised from the dead through the glory of the Father, we too may live a new life." Romans 6:3-4 (NIV)

I love to share this testimony about my mom. As a child, her grandpa was a Methodist Pastor and he sprinkled her in the titles of the Father, Son and Holy Ghost. When Mom was 24 years old, she got baptized by full immersion in the water, again in the titles of: The Father, Son, and Holy Ghost. The next few years, several strangers crossed her path telling her that God wanted to save her. Mom was getting annoyed by all these different people ministering to her, and was under the impression that she was already saved by confessing Christ as her Savior.

Mom crossed paths with a few others who insisted she needed to be re-baptized in the name of Jesus. The devil wanted to keep her walking in rebellion towards the truth and enslaved. At 28 years old, she was invited to an Apostolic-Pentecostal church. A former devout "Jehovah's Witness" co-worker who had gotten baptized in Jesus' name and filled with the Holy Spirit asked my mom to be her guest at her new church. At the close of the service, Mom was pushed down the aisle. She assumed her co-worker was forcing her to the front. Mom turned around abruptly to say, 'Get your hands off me!' No one was behind her and the lady was still at her seat. Mom realized that the invisible hand of God ushered her to the altar with such gentleness. Mom heard in a whisper, **"Eternity is too long to be wrong!"**

*"For as many of you as were baptized into **Christ** have put on Christ." Galatians 3:27 ESV*

My mother was practically ready to run and dive into the baptism pool at that point. She was then baptized for the 3rd time in the name of Jesus Christ. Afterward, Mom felt spiritually cleansed and recognized a distinct difference. Since the Lord pushed her down the aisle, there had to be a significance in her baptism being done correctly. "Eternity is too long to be wrong," certainly does not sound like something to take lightly. We pray over our food in the name of JESUS, demons are cast out in the name of JESUS, and we lay hands on the sick to be healed in the name of JESUS. Satan knows that the power is in the name of JESUS, so he will allow anyone to be baptized in "titles" and fail to call the NAME of JESUS.

Matthew 28:19, is one of the most misunderstood verses in the Bible. The command was to baptize in the *"name,"* which is <u>singular</u>. Jesus' instructions were *not* to use the titles of Father, Son, and Holy Spirit as a formula. **These nouns do not implement a name.** Jesus is the *"one name"* for all three titles.

*Then opened he their understanding, that they might understand the scriptures, And said unto them, Thus it is written, and thus it behooved Christ to suffer, and to rise from the dead the third day: **And that repentance and remission of sins should be preached in* <u>*his name*</u> *among all nations, beginning at Jerusalem.*
Luke 24:45-47

Father is JESUS
Jesus said, "I am come in my Father's name."
John 5:43

Jesus said, "Me and my Father are ONE."
John 10:30

Jesus answered: "Don't you know me, Philip, even after I have been among you such a long time? Anyone who has seen me has seen the Father. How can you say, 'Show us the Father?"
John 14:9 NIV

Son is JESUS

She will give birth to a son, and you are to give him the name Jesus, because he will save his people from their sins. Matthew 1:21 NIV

Holy Ghost is JESUS

"But the Helper, the Holy Spirit, whom the Father will send in My name, He will teach you all things, and bring to your remembrance all things that I said to you. " John 14:26 NKJV

God is the Father in creation, Son in redemption, and the Holy Ghost that dwells inside of us. Jesus is the *saving name,* and every knee will bow and every tongue will Confess that Jesus Christ is Lord (Acts 4:12, Phil. 2:10-11). Peter actually confirmed what was stated in Matthew 28:19 in Acts 2:38 by giving the name of those titles. All throughout the book of Acts, baptism was only performed in the name of the **Lord Jesus Christ.** The verses below support this as well.

"There is no other name under heaven given among men whereby we can be saved." Acts 4:12

*"Now when the apostles which were at Jerusalem heard that Samaria had received the word of God, they sent unto them Peter and John: Who, when they were come down, prayed for them, that they might receive the Holy Ghost: (For as yet he was fallen upon none of them: only they were **baptized** in the name of the **Lord Jesus**.)"* Acts 8:14-16

*Then answered Peter, Can any man forbid water, that these should not be baptized that received the Holy Ghost as well as we? And he commanded them to be **baptized** in the name of the **Lord**. "* Acts 10:48

*"When they heard this, they were **baptized** in the name of the Lord **Jesus**."* Acts 19:5

"And now what are you waiting for? Get up, be baptized and wash your sins away, calling on His name." Acts 22:16 NIV

*"Thou believest that there is **one** God; thou doest well: the devils also believe, and tremble."* James 2:19

The terms *Holy Ghost* and *Holy Spirit* mean exactly the same thing. The phrase Holy Ghost is simply an older term that is predominantly used in the King James Version. Considering the word *ghost* has a different meaning today than it did back then, modern translations of the Bible always use Holy Spirit.

The Holy Spirit is a necessity to live HOLY.

The Holy Spirit is your divine ability to take authority over demonic principalities. Without it, only having earnest intentions to walk with God will not stand against the pitfalls, persecution, and relentless seduction from the enemy. You might be able to utilize 'temporary willpower,' but you need the Holy Ghost POWER. Satan cannot interpret when a Believer speaks in tongues, so he tries to make people think it is not necessary. Acts 2 says everyone was filled, which means no one was overlooked.

*"And it shall come to pass in the last days, saith God I will pour out my Spirit upon **all flesh**: and your sons and daughters shall prophesy, and your young men shall see visions, and your old men shall dream dreams."* Acts 2:17

The Bible mentions a God-fearing man named Cornelius that gave food and money to the poor in Acts chapter ten. The Lord sent angels to both Peter and Cornelius in a vision with instructions on how to meet each other. Despite his good deeds he still needed to be saved. Peter preached the good news to Cornelius, his family, and friends.

*"While Peter spake these words, the Holy Ghost fell on all them which heard the word. And they of the circumcision (Jews) which believed were astonished, as many as came with Peter, because that on the Gentiles (non-Jews) also was poured out the **gift of the Holy Ghost**. For they heard them speak with **tongues**, and magnify God. Then answered Peter, Can any man forbid water, that these should not be baptized that received the Holy Ghost as well as we? And he commanded them to be **baptized** in the name of the **Lord**."* Acts 10:44-48

Receiving the Holy Ghost first did not make Cornelius and his household exempt from baptism. Remember, in John 3:5 Jesus said, *"You **must** be* born again of **water** and of **Spirit** or you **cannot enter the kingdom of God.**" When the Holy Spirit comes in, the tongues (heavenly language) will flow out. John 3:8 references, "*When the Spirit comes you will hear the sound thereof.*" God wants everyone to be filled with the Holy Spirit, and it is being poured out on ALL flesh (Joel 2:28, Acts 2:17).

When you speak in tongues for the first time, it is an encounter that will leave you speechless to describe. No one will be able to persuade you that God does not exist. It is a miracle to speak in a language that you were never taught. Every burden that you carry is released through your prayer language unto the Lord. "Now if any man has not the Spirit of Christ, he is none of His." Romans 8:9[b]

Some will dispute that because *the Thief on the Cross* beside Jesus was not baptized or filled with the Holy Spirit, it is not required. This assumption is false, due to the fact that the Crucifixion was still during the dispensation (period) of the *Law*. Jesus ascended into heaven (Acts 1:9), and sent back the gift of the Holy Spirit (Acts 2:1-4). The historical event spoken of in Acts 2 is the shift in time that placed us under GRACE on the Day of Pentecost. Salvation is a finished work of the cross that must be appropriated by obeying Acts 2:38.

"*The Jews had agreed already that if anyone confessed that He was Christ, he would be put out of the synagogue.*" John 9:22[b]

"That if thou shalt confess with thy mouth the Lord Jesus, and shalt believe in thine heart that God hath raised him from the dead, thou shalt be saved." Romans 10:9

In spite of being thrown out of the synagogue as stated in John 9:22; Jews have an obligation to verbally confess Jesus Christ as the Messiah in order to be saved. Several people misinterpret Romans 10:9, and are misled to believe this scripture is telling them how to get saved. Romans 1:7 states this letter is written to the saints in Rome. In the original Greek translation, the word for "confess" is homologeo which means to be repetitive in your speech. The Greek word sozo means saved and it is not defined as salvation, but rather to remain secure in your walk with the Lord admonishing Israel to forsake Mosaic ordinances. Chapters 9, 10, and 11 of Romans are written to Israel (Jews). God chose Jews for a task that is traced back to Abraham in Genesis. Later, they rebelled and also rejected Jesus as the Messiah. The context of these letters in Romans 9, 10, and 11 signifies only a remnant of Jews would be saved because of them rejecting Jesus.

The Plan of Salvation, from the Day of Pentecost until Jesus returns is found in Acts 2:38. The gospel spread abroad and other ministries were instituted. Consistent biblical documentation of water baptism in the name of Jesus Christ and speaking in tongues are found in: Acts 8:12-17, Acts 8:35-38, Acts 9:17-18, Acts 10:44-48, Acts 16:13-16 and Acts 16:33, and Acts 19:1-6.

In the New Testament, from Romans to Jude those letters are written to those of us who are already saved (the Body of Christ). As a whole, Epistles tend to deal with three general issues: doctrine, application, and logistics. By reading the Epistles we can also learn how to maintain our salvation, operate in giftings, keep order in the church, and look for Christ's appearing etc.

Introductory Greetings to Local Churches

-Rom. 1:7 To all that be in Rome, beloved of God, called to be saints
-1 Cor. 1:2 Unto the church of God which is at Corinth, to them that are sanctified in Christ Jesus, called to be saints
-2 Cor. 1:1 To the church of God which is at Corinth, with all the saints who are in all Achaia
-Gal. 1:2 To the churches of Galatia
-Eph. 1:1 To the saints who are in Ephesus, and faithful in Christ Jesus
-Phil. 1:1 To all the saints in Christ Jesus who are in Philippi, with the bishops and deacons
-Col. 1:2 To the saints and faithful brethren in Christ who are in Colosse
-1 Thess. 1:1-2, 2 Thess.1:1 To the church of the Thessalonians
-1 Tim. 1:2, 2 Tim. 1:2 To Timothy, a true son in the faith..... a beloved son
-Titus 1:4 To Titus, a true son in our common faith
-Philemon 1:1 To Philemon our beloved friend and fellow laborer
-Heb. 1:2 has in these last days spoken to us by His Son

-James 1:1 To the twelve tribes which are scattered abroad: Greetings
-1 Pet. 1:1 I am writing to God's chosen people
-2 Pet.1:1 I am writing to you who share the same precious faith we have.
-1 John 1:3 We proclaim to you what we ourselves have actually seen and heard so that you may have fellowship with us
-2 John 1:1 The elder unto the elect lady and her children, whom I love in the truth; and not I only, but also all they that have known the truth
-3 John 1:1 The elder unto the wellbeloved Gaius, whom I love in the truth.
-Jude 1:1 to them that are sanctified by God the Father, and preserved in Jesus Christ, and called
-Rev. 1:1 to shew unto his servants things which must shortly come to pass; and he sent and signified it by his angel unto his servant John

If you have never spoken in tongues, do not criticize what you have not experienced. I would encourage you to follow along with the instructions in the next chapter to receive the Holy Spirit. *"For he (satan) is a liar, and the father of it"* (John 8: 44 KJV). Jesus will not hurt you in this process of seeking to be filled with His Spirit. There have been occasions in which many have trusted people they barely knew. Since God created us, we should be at peace with trusting Him. John 3:5 is a mandate and Acts 2:38 is the fulfillment of it. Just obey it.

Remember the last words Jesus *spoke, "But ye shall receive power, **after** that the* Holy Ghost *is come upon you"* (Acts 1:8 KJV). Before receiving the

Holy Spirit, you have no spiritual authority. The Holy Spirit will equip you to live above sin's control.

If you need a church to baptize you in the name of JESUS, according to Acts 2:38, google Apostolic church with your zip code behind it or go to findyourlocalchurch.com and tap on your state and scroll down to your city. Also, another option is UPCI.org and type in your zip code.

You Shall Receive Power

Some are mistaking one of the 9 spiritual gifts called, *divers kinds of tongues* as being synonymous with the infilling of the Holy Spirit. To function in any of the 9 gifts listed in 1 Corinthians 12:1-11, you need the Holy Spirit with the initial evidence of speaking with other tongues. The operation of the gift of tongues is when a believer speaks in several languages.

"If ye then, being evil, know how to give good gifts unto your children: how much more shall your heavenly Father give the Holy Spirit to them that ask him?" Luke 11:13

Jesus stood and cried, saying, "If any man thirst, let him come unto me and drink. He that believeth on me, as the scripture hath said, out of his belly shall flow rivers of living water." John 7:37-38

There is no silent manifestation of receiving the Holy Spirit. Anytime someone was filled with the Holy Spirit in the book of Acts, they spoke in tongues. This is a supernatural language accompanied with power. Several misconstrue emotional encounters such as: goosebumps, crying, or a warm sensation as the infilling of the Holy Spirit. The presence of God is drawing an individual when they have these types of experiences. It definitely is an indication that God is dealing with a person and beckoning their attention.

"They were all filled with the Holy Ghost, and began to speak with other tongues, as the Spirit gave them utterance." Acts 2:4

Three barriers the enemy will use to stop you from being filled with the Holy Spirit are: unbelief, unforgiveness, and failure to repent. The Holy Spirit is a *gift and a promise.* God does not show favoritism. If he has given the Holy Spirit to others, you are not excluded. True repentance puts your heart in a position to be filled with the Holy Spirit.

Are you ready to get filled with the Holy Spirit? Trust God, do not be scared. He is not going to hurt you. The Lord is standing outside the door of your heart knocking to come in. Pray a brief sincere prayer of repentance, and conclude by asking the Lord Jesus to allow you to receive His Spirit.

As an expression of praise, you are going to repeatedly say aloud, "Thank you Jesus, thank you Jesus, thank you Jesus" (over and over do not stop praising Him). You are thanking Him in advance for the gift of the Holy Spirit, and all the other wonderful things He has done. You are not saying this to be repetitious like a robot. As you keep saying, "Thank You Jesus," it will become more difficult to keep repeating that praise. Keep up a momentous pace, which will prevent distractions from bombarding your mind. God dwells in the midst of praises. Keep praising him! "Thank you Jesus, thank you Jesus, thank you Jesus."

It may feel like you are getting tongue-tied and you are unable to say, " Thank you Jesus " so precisely. You will not be out of control or unaware of your surroundings. God is NOT going to make you speak, but you must yield to the Spirit. As you worship God from your heart, he will begin to transition you into another language. It all begins with sounds like when a baby is trying to talk they may say, "Goo goo, ga-ga ma ma da da." Your heavenly prayer language will start with small syllables.

Do not try to figure it out. If you hear in your mind some foreign sounds just speak them out. For example, when conversing with someone you are configuring your next response in your mind. You will not understand it.

You cannot speak two languages at the same time. Go with the change, when you are beginning to "stutter." Do not assume that because you have praised God repetitiously that you are stuttering or becoming tongue tied as a result; this is an indication that the Holy Spirit wants to speak through you. No matter what it sounds like, keep making those strange sounds. The more that you trust the Lord and continue speaking out this supernatural, unknown language it will advance from sounding like baby talk to a fluent dialect. *"But God has chosen the foolish things of the world to confound the wise,"* 1 Corinthians 1:27

The sounds will seem foreign to you. You will not understand what you are saying unless God gives you the interpretation. Your heavenly language will become clearer as you are speaking out the syllables. The Spirit of God is giving you what to say. The devil will make you think that you are making up something or sounding foolish. Allow the Holy Spirit to flow out of your belly, and by faith believe this is the Lord. Open and close your mouth the same way you do when having a regular conversation and listen to yourself speaking in tongues.

"For he that speaketh in an unknown tongue speaketh not unto men, but unto God: for no man understandeth him; howbeit in the spirit he speaketh mysteries." 1 Corinthians 14:2

Jesus loves you so much and he wants you to be empowered. You won't say anything wrong, just relax and keep speaking in tongues. Pronounce the words as if you would vowels A, E, I, O, U with your mouth constantly moving. You are not giving yourself the Holy Spirit; it is speaking through you as God gives the ability.

Praying in tongues allows you to pray directly to God from your spirit. This is your own personal language to communicate and be spiritually edified. You magnify and praise God from your spirit and pray the will of God.

New Creature

A stronghold is something that has been built over time.
-Bishop S.Y. Younger

I want to encourage you while adapting to a new lifestyle, not to condemn yourself behind any past mistakes. An 'overnight *deliverance'* in which one experiences immediate results very seldom happens. Of course, God's sovereignty can heal and remove sinful desires instantaneously, but many are regenerated as they go forward in their pilgrimage. Just as a newborn baby spits up and poops on itself, you as a *spiritual baby* will have some mishaps occur. Salvation is is separate from deliverance. Eliminating sin and adjusting to a new routine takes time. None of us will be perfect but as a Christian we are aiming to refrain from premeditated sin.

Do not dwell on the past it can make you depressed, and do not worry about the future you will become anxious. Take one day at a time!

Strategically, identify those things that have a negative influence or a hold on you. Hindrances will keep you from attaining your deliverance. It will become easier to live righteously when you pinpoint your short comings. A holy lifestyle is a decision that you must walk in daily.

It may be emotionally painful while taking action and walking through deliverance. However, the power of the Holy Spirit will break every chain. God's love will heal, and motivate you into a greater purpose.

There are different levels in the realm of the Spirit. You will reach your "Spiritual Peak," through obedience to God. Instead of concentrating on your struggle, fill every void with worship and prayer. If you truly desire for God to transform you, He will! God completely heals people's physical body, so why would he half-deliver you? Jeremiah 32:27 says, "Behold, I am the Lord, the God of all flesh: is there anything too hard for me?"

The word of God is a cleansing agent as it washes your mind, and conditions your heart. The book of Hebrews tells us that God's Word is alive and active (Hebrews 4:12). The Holy Spirit begins to work on the inner person, exposing your true thoughts and attitudes while reading the living Word. It takes the Word of God to reveal what is of the flesh. We all have some things that we need to eliminate and should not make excuses by reciting, 'This is who I am.'

As you read the Word, you must apply it to your life (James 1:22-24). God blesses total submission. We operate by a standard of holiness as we are transformed. *Jesus answered, "It is written: 'Man shall not live on bread alone, but on every word that comes from the mouth of God'"* (Matthew 4:4 NIV).

If the Lord sends you an accountability partner, do not become so accustomed with struggling it blocks you from receiving help. The devil thrives on darkness and shame. Having a spiritual confidant will prevent a wall of frustration. We will never be sinless in this life. *"If we say that we have no sin, we deceive ourselves, and the truth is not in us"* (1 John 1:8). When you surrender your will to God, your desires will evolve to reflect His nature and character. Your deliverance becomes more defined as you spiritually elevate.

"Run from anything that stimulates youthful lusts. Instead, pursue righteous living , faithfulness, love, and peace. Enjoy the companionship of those who call on the Lord with pure hearts." 2 Timothy 2:22 NLT

Becoming emotionally whole is an asset for growth. Letting go of grudges and past traumatic incidents, will alleviate your mind to envision your bright future. Forgiveness is the act of pardoning an offender. You must cease to feel resentment and forgive your enemies. It is absolutely mandatory to forgive in order to be delivered!

Deliverance only comes to the desperate and healing to the humble. The word of God teaches in 1 Corinthians 13:4-5 that unselfish love is the basis for true forgiveness, since love does not keep an account of the injury. Even more important, forgiving others is a key to receiving Christ's forgiveness for your own sins.

"If you forgive those who sin against you, your heavenly Father will forgive you. But if you refuse to forgive others, your Father will not forgive your sins." Matthew 6:14-15 NLT

Enduring the Process

"And do not be conformed to this world: but be ye transformed by the renewing of your mind, that ye may prove what is that **good** (30), and **acceptable** (60), and **perfect** (100) will of God." Romans 12:2

Deliverance is a 30, 60, and 100-fold progressive scale.

The Greek word Teknon, means "Just Born," which can be compared to **good** in the 30-fold stage of deliverance. As a new convert, you may still wrestle with learned behaviors. This is not a reason to give in to temptation or an excuse to revert back to your former lifestyle. Remain faithful to the Lord under pressure and He will gradually propel you. This is a spiritual fight. Struggling with certain habits or making a mistake, does not mean that you are unsaved.

In Greek lexicons, the word Huios is defined as, "One on the correct path of growth." As a growing Believer, this phase of deliverance is considered 60-fold, which equates to **acceptable**. Being able to obtain self-control and refrain from yielding to temptation is a huge success. When facing trials, you can expect God to also be with you through them. You are enjoying the fellowship of other Christians, and establishing a firm foundation in your personal relationship with Christ.

The proof of 100-fold total deliverance is when you no longer commit the same sins that you were involved in when you got saved. The adversary has to conjure up new strategies because you have outgrown those pitfalls. When you become **_perfect_,** it means mature, which is the Greek word Teleios. Your goal is two-fold; first reaching the level of transformation that no longer reflects your past, and secondly entering a place of satisfaction with who you are, and where you are.

A transforming of the mind in your thought process, responses, and presentation takes discipline. At this point, once you become totally delivered there is nothing in you that is contemplating reverting to the past. The residue is gone and what you do not want no one can make you indulge in again. The opposite of temptation is contentment. This is a dimension of being in God's perfect will. Your aim will be to please God, opposed to attempting to get away with premeditated sin.

Sin is a choice, not a necessity.

If I was able to go through this process after living as a transgender male for 20 years, I know you can do it! Do not ever feel that you are not worthy or capable of completing this journey if you fall into any sin. That is why baptism in the name of Jesus Christ is so vital because it washes away the sins you committed, and covers any future mistakes in the Blood of Jesus.

As a new convert you just have to take one day at a time. We can be our biggest enemy at times. You must make a sound decision to save yourself from yourself. Doing things in our flesh has resulted in hitting a dead-end wall. Only what we do for Christ will last.

Let's explore a butterfly's life cycle in detail. All butterflies experience a **"complete metamorphosis."** To grow into their final creation, they go through 4 stages: egg, larva, pupa, and adult. Each stage has a different goal. You are going to be amazed by your own transformation as God molds you into a beautiful new creature.

Whatever you have to give up is going to be worth it!

1st Stage-Egg- A butterfly starts life as a very small, round, or oval egg. The coolest thing about butterfly eggs, is that if you look close enough you can see the tiny caterpillar growing inside of it. The egg shape depends on the type of butterfly that laid the egg.

Your decision to turn your back on sin is a very courageous choice. Do not forget that we all start somewhere. This process may seem scary but do it afraid. In society, we cannot escape a sinful environment. However, please take into consideration what you entertain. Watching sexual scenes on TV, hearing explicit lyrics in music, entertaining people who gossip or use tons of profanity is not helping your purification process, and will contaminate your Spirit.

The devil will attack your mind to take you backward into bondage. Demons not only attack your mind, but your memory, thought pattern, and the things you see. If he cannot get you to think about going back, then he will try to get you to see that which is behind you to pull you back. Satan's third trick, is to assign a *person* to stop your growth. Stay alert and remain determined. As my leader Bishop Younger says, "Before you decide to give up, take into consideration that this time next year you will be happy that you kept going!"

Do not let the devil make you feel like these per-cautions are extreme. One must re-evaluate routine habits and replace them with new attributes. If you need to change your phone number to avoid temptation do what you feel necessary. As a "New Creature" you want to create new memories that will glorify God.

Conversing with unsaved friends can become a distraction used by the adversary to keep you focused on the past. If the Holy Spirit urges you to avoid traps by disconnecting from certain people; it may cause you to feel sentimental, nevertheless it is all a part of the 'growing pains.' The updates associated with your past will deceive you into thinking you are missing out on something and coerce you back into a sinful lifestyle. A person may not be aware that they are being a bad influence, but do not be fooled by the devil's schemes. Focus on yourself!

Anyone that indulges in a worldly lifestyle of sin may tell you it is unnecessary to change. Sometimes others are intrigued by your personality, so they are afraid of losing that bond. Steer clear of that kind of phony validation. I am advising you to disassociate from old friends from experience. I stayed in contact with an old buddy in 2002 in hopes of him getting saved but instead he drew me back into darkness.

"Bad company corrupts good character." **1 Corinthians 15:33 NLT**

You should cut ties with ex-lovers or sexual partners. Staying connected is a soul-tie and will keep alive a spirit of lust within your emotions. Do not think that their salvation is based upon your evangelism. If the Holy Spirit is drawing them, your assistance is unnecessary to win them to Christ. There are millions of Believers who the Lord can cross their paths with to share the gospel. Familiarity can cause you to remain in a vicious cycle.

Unusual distress is caused from significant life changes while detaching from people, places, or articles.

"Let us strip off every weight that slows us down, especially the sin that so easily trips us up. And let

us run with endurance the race God has set before us." Hebrews 12:1 NLT

Renunciations are defined as a definite way that you refuse to follow, obey, or support something any longer. You are making a declaration, which relinquishes the legal access of the enemy serving him an eviction notice. Death and life are in the power of the tongue (Proverbs 18:21). Renunciations play a *significant* part in the DELIVERANCE process!

I want to emphasize that the renunciations must be said *out loud*, and not read silently. Remember, this is to exercise your authority through your voice because victory produces a sound. You must say these renunciations with fervency. If any manifestation of demonic spirits causes you to vomit or cough up phlegm, keep calling on the name of Jesus and commanding the devil to go in Jesus name!!!

Say aloud, "I renounce soul ties in the name of Jesus. I renounce all spirits of lust that are interlocked with the occult in the name of Jesus. I renounce perversion which entails: role-playing, lesbianism, fornication, pornography,adultery, masturbation, and fantasy in the name of Jesus.

I renounce and command all spirits of impurity, lust, and perversion, to come out of my mind, will, and emotions in the name of Jesus. I break all curses of molestation, rape, incest, promiscuity, and perversion in the mighty name of Jesus. I renounce and cast out thoughts of shame, condemnation, unworthiness, and guilt in the name of Jesus. I renounce all strongholds to alcohol, drugs, and any illegal substance in the name of Jesus.

I command all spirits that would make me feel lonely and desperate for a companion to flee now in the name of Jesus. I command all spirits of incubus, and succubus to come out of my sexual organs in the name of Jesus. *(incubus and succubus are sexual night demons that arouse you in your sleep). *

I renounce all spirits of hurt, rejection, depression, anger, retaliation, fear, grief, bitterness, unforgiveness, anxiety, confusion, and hopelessness to loose my will, emotions, and mind in the name of Jesus. I renounce and command any addictive personality that I have inherited to come out of my appetite in the name of Jesus. I renounce any generational spirits of lust in my bloodline in the name of Jesus.

I renounce all spirits of narcissism, arrogance, ego, stubbornness, pride, disobedience, rebellion, self-will, and denial in the name of Jesus. I forgive any person that has offended, abused, caused distress, rejected, or abandoned me in the name of Jesus. I command any spirit that I am unaware of that is active in my life to come out in the name of Jesus.

I declare and decree my breakthrough and prophesy that I will not keep struggling with this demonic spirit of perversion in the name of JESUS! As I delight myself in the Lord, my desires will change. I am totally FREE in the name of Jesus Christ!"

"Greater is HE that is in me than he that is in the world." 1 John 4:4

The Lord wants you to experience genuine joy. I speak over your life total deliverance, and blessings in the mighty name of JESUS CHRIST! You will not go back to a lifestyle of habitual sin. The Holy Ghost will guide you into a pathway of righteousness.

How can you be who you were and who you are at the same time? You cannot surround yourself with the same spirits that you want to get delivered from. A sheep cries if they get stuck in some mud, but a pig will wallow in it. The prodigal son in Luke 15:11-32 realized that he was living beneath his privilege while eating what he fed to the pigs. We have natural and spiritual benefits when we follow Christ.

The glory of the future is the joy of the present.

You must be consistent with your attendance at church. The devil attempts to use self-doubt to make you feel inadequate. Some anxiety may occur as you are in between transitioning. Do not feel as though you do not fit the criteria of other men/women in the congregation. The House of

God is for everyone and the blood of Jesus was shed for all of humanity.

The Lord knows how to bless you with new friends in due season. Your life has already been planned from start to finish. God is in divine control and has promised to be alongside you every step of the way. Faith is when you place your trust in God although the outcome is not visible. We can't even please God if we do not believe that he is able to do the things that we think are impossible. The battlefield of the mind is a force to reckoned with, but keep thinking on things that are uplifting and optimistic. The less attention that you give to negative thoughts, the more joy you will obtain. Some chatter is not even worth addressing, it is simply an attack to distract.

2nd Stage Caterpillar- When the egg finally hatches, most of you would expect for a butterfly to emerge, right? Well, not exactly. In the butterfly's life cycle, this is only the second stage. Butterfly larvae are what we call caterpillars. When they start eating, they instantly start growing and expanding.

God promises that He will liberate us through prayer and fasting. It means the voluntary abstinence from food. Keep fasting however long it takes for you to get your breakthrough. I do not mean to starve yourself and never eat again until you are delivered. What I am suggesting, is to fast "consistently" 2 to 3 days out the week during certain hours for an extensive period of time.

Fasting tears down the wall of the flesh and causes you to maintain a healthy attitude.
-Apostle JW Webster

On the days that you choose to fast, only drink liquids and eat one meal for dinner. Please do not follow these fasting guidelines if you have health challenges that will not permit you to go without food, or you are taking medication that requires a meal with dosages. Instead, refrain from other things or activities that you enjoy such as: coffee, candy, social media, unnecessary phone conversations, television, or other comforts unrelated to food.

"And he (Jesus) said unto them, this kind can come forth by nothing, but by prayer and fasting." Mark 9:29

"Is not this the fast that I have chosen? to loose the bands of wickedness, to undo the heavy burdens, and to let the oppressed go free, and that ye break every yoke?" Isaiah 58:6

In my case, I fasted every Monday, Wednesday, and Friday for 9 months. On top of practicing a 20-year lifestyle of homosexuality, I had addictions to drugs and alcohol that needed to be destroyed. I did not want a *temporary* relief nor did I want for these strongholds to *play dead* in my life. Instead, I wanted these things to be uprooted from the core of my being.

If you are single, your sexual desires will become intense as you begin to starve them. The activity of that spirit of lust/perversion is going to tempt you with suggestions to satisfy your flesh. <u>Strongholds lose its strength while you are fasting.</u> Prayer and fasting cause the spirit of God to be resurrected, and purge you with a refining fire, which pushes these opposing spirits out. You cannot receive the promises of God with a carnal (fleshly) mentality. Desiring to live holy will become beneficial in your spiritual walk.

Fasting, prayer, and depositing the word of God into your Spirit are the most important tools of deliverance. Empowerment flows when you exercise your spiritual resources. You will grab God's attention through making a sacrifice to refrain from food. God will set us free from being affected by what others think, making us realize that any comparison we make with others is a guaranteed fast track to misery. If you have never fasted before, ease into it slowly. Begin by skipping one or two daily meals; replace food with prayer and worship. I suggest reading Bible verses in Proverbs to teach you about Godly wisdom.

You can begin doing a partial fast from 8 AM until Noon twice a week. Then after you become accustomed to partially fasting, you can begin fasting from Midnight until 2 PM twice a week. During the hours of fasting listen to worship music, study a few scriptures, and pray in tongues. A suggestion would be to fast on your days off from work. If you choose to fast while working, use your lunch break to pray and read scriptures.

After a month or so increase your fasting to 3 times a week Midnight until 3 PM, then gradually start going until 4 PM. At times, the Lord may lead you to do a 3 day fast that permits only liquids, fruits, and vegetables. The objective is to fast until the stronghold of sins such as: cursing, porn, masturbation, drug/alcohol addictions etc. disconnect from the soulish realm. The relationship you are establishing with God will begin to transform your countenance.

Our 21st century culture can lead us to becoming numb to what matters to God. Jesus did not waver as to whether His church would fast. *"When you fast,"* He said — not "if" (Matthew 6:16-17). As you detox the spirit and become consumed with desire and praise for God, you become sensitive to His voice.

When you acknowledge through fasting that you need God to *live,* and to live more abundantly, you will begin to desire God in a new way. Realizing you need God more than food, will make you appreciative of what the Psalmist meant when he wrote, "Like the deer that pants after water, my soul longs for You" (Psalm 42:1). His purpose and plan are totally different from your will and your way.

Pace yourself and if you have to concentrate on one thing at a time that is perfectly fine.

Whatever reminds you of the past in a negative sense or a portal of temptation just eliminate it. The Holy Spirit is not going to lead you to discard things which He will not replace in a greater magnitude. The will of God is accomplished through obedience. Ouija boards, tarot cards, energy crystals, chakra, mobile apps that are used for casual sexual hook-ups, explicit photos etc should be discarded/deleted.

Prayer has power over everything. Exercising faith produces a confident prayer life in which you believe that God hears your prayers and will answer them. Your communication with God is going to strengthen you day by day. Prayer is not always asking God for something. You cannot pray selfishly and expect Godly results. Sometimes it's an expression of feelings released toward the Lord as if you are speaking directly to a friend in front of you. God is an invisible being. It may seem like he is far away, but His Word declares that He will never leave or forsake you (Hebrews 13:5). Sometimes we just need to thank Him while praying, and worship Him for who He is. Worship removes the struggle of toiling with demonic forces.

A strong prayer life also will impart inner strength, wisdom, understanding, guidance, spiritual gifts, fullness of joy, peace, freedom from anxiety and fear. The power to change a situation is contingent upon how you perceive yourself. When your passion for God engulfs your heart, it is expressed in your prayers. When you recognize blessings being showered upon you that you did not deserve, it makes you thankful. The Lord gave us a guideline on how to address His throne. I believe the Lord's Prayer is a wonderful daily prayer to begin each day.

"After this manner therefore pray ye: Our Father which art in heaven, Hallowed be thy name. Thy kingdom come, Thy will be done in earth, as it is in heaven. Give us this day our daily bread. And forgive us our debts, as we forgive our debtors. And lead us not into temptation, but deliver us from evil: For thine is the kingdom, and the power, and the glory, forever. Amen." Matthew 6:9-13

"The effectual fervent prayer of a righteous man availeth much." James 5:19 [b]

Affirmations are a recipe for success. Look in the mirror and encourage yourself. Verbally confess that you are beautiful and regardless of how you feel today your future is brighter tomorrow. As you allow the Lord to beautify the meek with salvation, you become more than a conqueror (Ps. 149:4, Rom. 8:37).

Your Spirit becomes fueled as your relationship with God is solidified. The inside must be targeted, so that it can parallel with the transformation of cleansing the heart. After changing your appearance, you still have to work on eliminating old characteristics. The glory of God will reflect the outward as the inward is cultivated.

Talking to a therapist is a wonderful addition to incorporate with your spiritual regeneration to help you heal from past hurts.

On your pathway of deliverance, you are replacing the old lifestyle with new ambitions. Get rid of clothing that do not display Godly character. You might have to take a few days to bag up the items to balance out feeling overwhelmed. You will experience separation anxiety, but that is normal. Being accustomed to the routine of your former way of life was a comfort zone, so not knowing what is ahead can be scary in your natural mind. *"For God has not given us a spirit of fear, but of power and of love and of a sound mind"* (2 Timothy 1:7 NKJV).

Please do not allow yourself to feel flustered with *do's and don'ts.* You are on the Potter's wheel being shaped into a new creature (Jeremiah 18:1-10). Steadily begin to gravitate toward these suggestions as constructive criticism for your *deliverance* to be complete. The hand of God will not steer you in the wrong direction.

This advice is not to make you feel paranoid but provoke awareness of things you do not realize as a result of long-term habits.

"Therefore, if any man be in Christ, he is a new creature: old things are passed away; behold, all things are become new." 2 Corinthians 5:17

3rd Stage Chrysalis- A remarkable transformation in the third stage is taking place within the chrysalis (pupa) called metamorphosis. This is how the beautiful parts that make up the butterfly will emerge. From the outside of the cocoon, it looks as if the caterpillar may be resting, but the inside is where all the action is. The caterpillar is rapidly changing. Tissue, limbs, and organs of a caterpillar have all been changed by the time the pupa is finished and is now ready for the final stage of a butterfly's life cycle.

Walking in the divine purpose that God orchestrated for your life welcomes great favor. Obedience and submission will produce bountiful blessings. The Lord Jesus loves you and is walking every step of this journey with you.

A child of God conducts their self with class. Your goal is to *look* different (stylish but not bizarre), *sound* different (sober-minded), and master your *actions (self-control)*. It will be a challenge but rewarding in the end. Block out the accusations from the adversary who will make you feel reluctant.

Now let's discuss the key role that sanctification plays in your spiritual growth. Sanctify means to be separate or to be set apart. The Lord desires us to be free to live without condemnation. We are no longer held hostage by satan. Sanctification does not stop after obeying Acts 2:38. It is a progressive process that continues, so that through it we may be blessed.

You must realize the opposition is between your old sinful character and new Spirit-man attributes. The heart's desire is to obey God, but our flesh is weak making sin difficult to resist. Yet, it is in the continual struggle with sin and obedience to God that sanctification does its work.

"For the flesh lusts against the Spirit, and the Spirit against the flesh; and these are contrary to one another, so that you do not do the things that you wish." Galatians 5:17 NKJV

Sanctification can be described as an inward spiritual process whereby God brings about purity and change by means of the Holy Spirit. We all face different issues that hinder our ability to live the life God desires for us. Our Spirit begins to convict us about areas that need to be corrected, helping us to evolve in our lifestyle of holiness. We become cognizant of our actions, surroundings, and associations from a more biblical perspective.

Just because it's difficult doesn't mean it's not destiny. Your destiny is not linked to your comfortability, your destiny is linked to God's will. -Bishop SY Younger

As you are being redefined you may feel lonely. God is omnipresent, meaning everywhere at the same time. This isolation period will strengthen you for your lifetime commitment to Christ. You are God's masterpiece. He is so proud of your growth. When you feel forgotten you are not; you have a personal angel assigned to you.

Praying in tongues is edifying to your spirit and intercedes on behalf of God's will. It is the highest form of the prayer of agreement, and it empowers you to subdue the desires of the flesh. There is a relief from anxiety and stress when you stir up the gift of your heavenly language. The Holy Spirit will perform a surgery within your emotions by healing past disappointments and pitfalls experienced throughout life. Sometimes I would lay beside my bed speaking in tongues so long that I would fall asleep in the presence of the Lord.

4th Stage Butterfly- Finally, when the caterpillar has done all its forming and changing inside the cocoon, you will get to see an adult butterfly emerge. When the butterfly exits from the chrysalis, it will pump blood into the wings in order to get them working and flapping – then they get to fly.

You have elevated into a new dimension; it is your time to fly. The glory of the Lord is illuminating from your countenance. You are a specimen of God's grace. You are loved by the Creator of all things, and you have been abiding in the Vine of His Presence.

Nothing about your character reflects the past. Your actions have become a normal routine and not calculated. The spirit of holiness has been imparted and is outwardly visible. You are content with your new identity and embracing it joyfully.

"I will give thanks to You, for I am fearfully and wonderfully made; Wonderful are Your works, and my soul knows it very well." Psalm 139:14 NASB

Continue to take one day at a time. Do not slack up on your prayer life. Commit to a day of fasting at least every other week. Your level of discipline over your flesh and temptation is measured by your lifestyle and consecration. Stay in fellowship with mature Christians to keep you accountable. He that has begun a good work will perform it until the day of Jesus Christ. Let your light shine that men may see your good works and glorify our Father in heaven. Godliness with contentment is great gain (Phil. 1:6, Matt. 5:18, 1 Tim. 6:6).

Whatever is valuable should be protected.

If you are single, please do not date someone that hasn't obeyed Acts 2:38. Just because they profess to be a Christian doesn't mean they are saved. Remember water baptism in the name of Jesus Christ and being filled with the Holy Spirit is essential. Ask them specifically if they have ever "spoke in tongues" because anyone will agree that they have the Holy Spirit. Some are erroneously taught that when they 'accept Christ' that the Holy Spirit enters their heart but that is not biblical. Reminder: When the Holy Spirit was poured out at Pentecost they ALL spoke in tongues (Acts 2:4).

"Two cannot walk together unless they are agreed." Amos 3:3

Being attracted to a person does not mean you are necessarily compatible. Ladies you do not want to follow a spiritually shallow man. You should be able to zip yourself up inside of him as a covering. Also, in a relationship it is important to have some things in common such as interests or hobbies. For example, if you like going on vacations or movie dates, but he is uninterested in being outdoors, it may be a conflict of interest later.

My 1st priority would be a man's spirituality. You also want to have chemistry with this person, which I would categorize as the 3rd component. I am not encouraging pre-marital sex, but the physical attraction should be present. However, sex can get old and undesirable if other dynamics are not flowing. The wisest decision while dating is to stay in a public setting. Many fall into fornication by putting too much confidence in their flesh entertaining at each others house or in cozy intimate environments. A respectful Godly gentleman or woman would never coerce you into having sex before marriage. Proverbs 6:27 says, "Can a man embrace fire and not be burned?"

I am just giving examples how to weigh out the odds. Personally, I view marriage as becoming one. You cannot get married with a single mentality or refusal to submit. I rather have more in common than not. Personally, I like to win souls and minister, so I would be attracted to a man who is just as passionate for God. If he loves God, I can be assured that he will love me as Christ loved the church (Eph. 5:25).

Keep a balanced life, and make sure that what you think is discernment is not fear or paranoia either. God has great things in store! Keep flapping those wings of freedom and shining on the winning team for Jesus! Remember this, the enemy is going to test your deliverance, but as you remain in prayer and studying the Word of God your strength to resist temptation will lift up a standard.

Fly High as God exceeds your expectations!

Walking Out Your Future

It is your responsibility to maintain your relationship with God. Attending church once a week on Sunday is not enough to keep you grounded. Your spiritual lifeline is contingent upon your application of the word. You do not want to complete this process and then get snatched backed into darkness. Do not to put yourself in a position to be tempted. Peradventure you fall into sin 1 John 1:9 says, *"If you confess your sins, He is faithful and just to forgive you and to cleanse you of all unrighteousness."*

Build a relationship with God that makes you refrain from sin because of the love you have for Him.

Please do not feel discouraged or defeated if you followed these steps, but still struggle with the temptation to commit sins from your past. Some may take longer than others to reach that realm in the Spirit. Struggling with a stronghold is not going to send you to hell. However, practicing sin or endorsing others who indulge (Eph. 5:7) will cast you into the lake of fire (Rev. 21:7-8). The consistency of your spiritual walk and discipline will peel off the layers of bondage like an onion. God is able!

Society has embraced sinful lifestyles and labeled it as the norm. If you take on that mindset, you will settle for spiritual mediocrity. The devil is the "father of lies" (John 8:44). The Word of God houses numerous deliverance's and healing's, but there was some type of action behind them. Keep confessing that you are delivered. Put your faith into motion. If you still have a few challenges but people can recognize your life is evolving, do not hesitate to testify of God's goodness. Your internal conflict will be eradicated as you stay the course. There is power and total deliverance in the name of JESUS Christ!

"Behold, I am the LORD, the God of all flesh: is there anything too hard for me?" Jeremiah 32:27

Healthy food is sold at grocery stores, but everyone does not choose to eat food with proper nutrients. Fitness gyms are global, but many will not join. In the same manner, you must fight for your freedom. Deliverance must be sought after. Some become satisfied at a 30 or 60-fold progression and make excuses for their back n' forth struggles. This does not have to be your permanent posture.

Even if you do not experience a change of feeling, you should not conclude that this is who you are, or just act upon what you feel. You must allow the Holy Spirit to rule over your flesh. Eat the word of God and let it resonate in your Spirit. Exercise faith to believe that your full 100-fold manifestation is coming! Keep fasting, praying, and attending church. I guarantee you one day the desires will cease. Steve Harvey made a valid point while sharing his testimony about living in his car.

He said, "The only way the possibility remains that it can happen, is if you never give up, no matter what you have to remain faithful."

Jesus healed many on the spot, while others improved as they went. Full deliverance is available for everybody because God is no respecter of persons, meaning he does not show favoritism. What God does for one, He will do for another. I can only speak from experience. These steps worked personally for me, and through abiding in the secret place of prayer/fasting in the cocoon, I was purged inwardly from unnatural desires, lust, addictions, etc.

"And from the days of John the Baptist until now the kingdom of heaven suffereth violence, and the violent take it by force." Matthew 11:12

An article in the Full Life Study Bible expounds on Matthew 11:12 saying, "The kingdom of heaven is taken hold of only by forceful people who are committed to breaking away from sinful and immoral lifestyles. No matter what may be the cost, such people vigorously seek the kingdom in all its power. Turning to Christ, His Word, and His righteous ways are the pathway of peace. In other words, experiencing the kingdom of heaven and all its blessings requires earnest endeavor. This is a fight of faith, accompanied by a strong will to resist satan, sin, and one's perverse society."

You cannot be a person that seldomly prays, compromises with the world, neglects the Word of

God, and has little spiritual hunger and succeed in your new walk. Brothers, read about some of the men of character and integrity in the Bible such as: Joseph (Gen. 39:9), Nathan (2 Sam. 12:7), Elijah (1 Ki. 18:21), Daniel and his 3 friends (Dan. 1:8, 3:16-18), Mordecai (Esth. 3:4-5), Peter and John (Acts 4:19-20), Stephen (Acts 6:8, 7:51), and Paul (Phil. 3:13-14). To name a few women of influence were: Deborah (Judges 4:9), Ruth (Ruth 1:16-18), Esther (Esth. 4:16), Mary (Luke 1:26-35), Anna (Luke 2:36-38), and Lydia (Acts 16:14-15,40). If the whole world is doing what is wrong, do not let that deter you.

A child of God should strive to live holy even if they are alone and embrace the unknown.

Read scriptures aloud in your leisure time. *"So then faith comes by hearing, and hearing by the word of God"* (Romans 10:17). Continuing to exercise your prayer life is going to keep you immersed in His presence. I understand that you may get sidetracked every once in a while, and might slack up on your studying, fasting, and praying. Instead of remaining in that place of distraction, get back in step as if you were in a marching band. Fall back in sync. Repent daily and ask for God's forgiveness of anything that you are aware or even unaware of.

"Pray without ceasing." 1 Thessalonians 5:17

We must put on the whole "ARMOR OF GOD" to stand against the tricks, schemes, and strategies of the enemy. The armor symbolizes the combat equipment of a Christian soldier who fights against spiritual wickedness. These are the resources that are available to all of us who decide to follow Christ. No one is exempt from the attacks of the devil now that we have chosen to serve the Lord.

"A final word: Be strong in the Lord and in his mighty power. Put on all of God's armor so that you will be able to stand firm against all strategies of the devil. For we are not fighting against flesh-and-blood enemies, but against evil rulers and authorities of the unseen world, against mighty powers in this dark world, and against evil spirits in the heavenly places. Therefore, put on every piece of God's armor so you will be able to resist the enemy in the time of evil. Then after the battle you will still be standing firm. Stand your ground, putting on the belt of truth and the body armor of God's righteousness. For shoes, put on the peace that comes from the Good News so that you will be fully prepared. In addition to all of these, hold up the shield of faith to stop the fiery arrows of the devil. Put on salvation as your helmet, and take the sword of the Spirit, which is the word of God. Pray in the Spirit at all times and on every occasion. Stay alert and be persistent in your prayers for all believers everywhere." Ephesians 6:10-18 NLT

We are instructed to "put on" this armor, which implies that we are not automatically suited in it. Putting on the armor of God requires a decision on our behalf. When armor is abused or worn incorrectly, it can malfunction. An in-depth explanation of the weaponry mentioned in the above passage of scripture is listed below.

Belt- Ancient Roman soldier's loins (waist) were girt about with a leather belt, which provided a place for the soldier's sword. Does our conviction to the truth encompass us? Scripture notes, truth must be bound around us and written on our hearts — our conviction must reach beyond an outward show. The belt represents TRUTH. John 17:17 says, *"Sanctify them by Your truth. Your word is truth."* The devil is a liar, and sometimes his lies sound like the truth. We must have the word of truth, which is the knowledge of God's word. Our spiritual belt of truth through studying the scriptures will keep us equipped to combat the enemies lies. If we hide His word in our hearts it will keep us from falling into premeditated sin (Psalm 119:11).

Breastplate of Righteousness- A soldier wore a breastplate made of bronze to cover the vital organs, especially the heart. This body armor represents a holy character and conduct. The devil often attacks our heart which is the seat of our emotions, self-worth, and trust. As we wear the breastplate of righteousness, we begin to allow our actions to reflect the purity of our heart. God's righteousness protects our heart from emotional injuries. *Guard your heart with all diligence* (Proverbs 4:23). When you know better, you will do better.

Sword- A soldier must be trained to effectively use his sword. As soldiers in God's ARMY we should study to show ourselves approved (2 Tim 2:15). This is why memorizing Scripture and becoming sensitive to the leading of the Holy Spirit is vital. The Holy Spirit uses the power of the Word to save souls and then to give them spiritual strength to be mature soldiers for the Lord in fighting this corrupt and evil world we live in.

The sword can also be used as a defensive weapon to protect us from the lies of the enemy. When we know the truth, we are able to defend against his lies. Each time satan tempted Jesus, He responded with the truth of Scripture. The word of God is alive, and powerful (Hebrews 4:12 KJV). There is power in the word of God, and we need to use our weapons against the wiles of the enemy. The scriptures make the devil nervous, and the name of Jesus will make him flee.

"The weapons of our warfare are not carnal but they are mighty through God to the pulling down of strongholds." 2 Corinthians 10:4-6

Shoes- Going to war without shoes it is most likely as a soldier walks over all kinds of harsh landscape it would inhibit his ability to fight. The word "gospel" means good news, referring to the sacrifice Jesus made for us so that we can be saved. As a result, this brings us peace. Having our feet fitted with the shoes of the gospel of peace allows us to be ready to share God with others at all times. As Christians, we should always be prepared, as we never know when an opportunity may arise to spread the good news of the gospel with someone else. Ultimately, the shoes of peace equip us to fight for Christ in the spiritual battles we face.

Shield of Faith- The Roman shield was as large as a door and would cover the warrior entirely. Shields, often made of wood and then covered in hide, when wet, could extinguish flaming arrows. The things Satan attempts to use to discourage us can actually become tools in the hands of God.

Faith is a protective barrier between us and the strategies of satan, and is our shield. No weapon formed against us will prosper (Isaiah 54:17). The attacks of the enemy will be thwarted by the shield of faith, and protect us from the fiery arrows.

"Everyone born of God overcomes the world. This is the victory that has overcome the world, even our faith." 1 John 5:4 NIV

Helmet- When a soldier suited up for battle, the helmet was the last piece of armor to go on. It was the final act of readiness in preparation for combat. The helmet was worn to protect the Warrior's head from physical blows in a battle. The head is the most vulnerable part of the body.

The greatest battlefield is in the mind. You cannot control your thoughts, but you have the ability to choose what you will meditate on. The devil has no new strategies so he will keep using the same traps repetitively. Remember as stated earlier demonic forces will attack your mind to take you backward into bondage. Demons not only attack your mind, but your memory, thought pattern, and visual images. If he cannot get you to think about going back, then he will try to get you to see that which is behind you to pull you back. Satan's third trick, is to assign a *person* to stop your growth, which is a distraction to your mind and destined purpose.

There are several actions a believer can take to keep this helmet fastened. Romans 12:1-2 instructs us to renew our minds by allowing the truth of God's Word to dismiss anything contrary to it. We must allow God's truth to continually wash away the world's twisted ideology, lies, and confusion from our minds and adopt God's perspective. Reject disbelief that arise from circumstances. It is impossible to have faith and doubt at the same time. God rewards our faith. With the helmet of salvation firmly in place, we can choose to believe what appears impossible (Heb. 11:6, 1 Pet. 1:8–9).

Remember that victory is already accomplished. When we consider ourselves "dead to sin but alive to God" (Romans 6:11), we eliminate many of the opportunities satan uses to entrap us. When choosing sin is no longer an option for us because we recognize ourselves to be "new creatures" we effectively cut off all avenues of failure (2 Corinthians 5:17; 1 John 3:9).

As we wear the helmet of salvation every day, our minds become more insulated against the suggestions, desires, and traps the enemy lays for us. We choose to guard our minds from excessive worldly influence and instead think on things that honor Christ (Philippians 4:8). In doing so, we wear our salvation as a protective helmet that will "guard our hearts and minds in Christ Jesus" (Philippians 4:7, Isaiah 26:3, 1 Peter 1:5).

Your focus is not necessarily the friends from the past, "all souls" need salvation. A recovered drug addict would not go into a crack house to share the gospel with old buddies. When you are converted strengthen your brothers (Luke 22:32). In my experience, God usually sends people who want to be delivered from homosexuality that I have no history with. Those who are serious, gladly receive the good news about Jesus Christ without opposition. Otherwise

Creating an atmosphere of devotion and praise shuts down the enemy. Devotion is an expression unto God of thankfulness, adoration, and joy. The Word will not return void, so keep quoting God's Word. The power of the Holy Spirit allows us to speak things into existence according to God's will for our lives. Praying in tongues keeps you strong, makes intercession on your behalf as well as others, and releases stress at the feet of the Father.

Let your objective be to represent the Lord with integrity. Regulate your thoughts, and actions through the word of God. Strive to reflect the nature of God inasmuch as we are made in his image. Allow the "Fruit of the Spirit" to fully operate through your life (Galatians 5:22-23). Faith in God's word is the greatest defense against the devil.

Keep your flesh in subjection by walking in humility. Pride goeth before destruction, and a haughty spirit before a fall (Prov. 16:18 KJV). Stay disengaged from old habits that are learned behavior. Fasting one day at least every other week will help your Spirit man stay reinforced. Also, consecration does not necessarily mean to refrain from eating. Get in the routine of reading the Bible for an hour and praying for an hour. It will take practice to reach that length of time but make it a goal.

Jesus said, "If any of you wants to be my follower, you must give up your own way, take up your cross daily, and follow me." Luke 9:23 NLT

Being discipled under a Bible-based, Spirit-filled church is necessary. It is dangerous to be a wandering sheep. Keep yourself submitted to a Pastoral leader. It is important to be accountable! The adversary loves to isolate you. You should pray about any decision, even if it seems minor. One wrong small decision, can result in bigger consequences later. Never think you know it all. It is wise to run things by people who are spiritual. In the multitude of counsel there is safety (Proverbs 11:14).

"Those who belong to Christ Jesus have nailed the passions and desires of their sinful nature to his cross and crucified them there." Galatians 5:24 NLT

"I am the vine; you are the branches. Whoever abides in me and I in him, he it is that bears much fruit, for apart from me you can do nothing."
John 15:5 ESV

Your best days are ahead! Remember, spiritual maintenance is essential. Rotate days to fast. Pray and read the bible regularly. I suggest Psalms and Proverbs to establish a routine. As you get used to studying, go over to some of the shorter letters written to Christians which are: Galatians, Ephesians, Philippians, and Colossians. Congratulations on a new life!!!

Questions

What areas of growth do you see in yourself after following the steps in this manual?

_____

_____

_____

_____

_____

_____

_____

_____

_____

_____

_____

Express the challenges of eliminating "learned behaviors." Do you realize that reprogramming your actions becomes natural after consciously taking the initiative to act upon them?

_____

_____

_____

_____

_____

_____

_____

_____

_____

_____

_____

_____

_____

_____

While going through your process of deliverance have you been able to pinpoint negative influences or surroundings to steer clear of?

_____

_____

_____

_____

_____

_____

_____

_____

_____

_____

_____

_____

_____

Do you feel like you have dominion over sin and leverage to make the right choices after receiving the baptism of the Holy Spirit? (speaking in tongues: Acts 2:4, Acts 2:38)

_____

_____

_____

_____

_____

_____

_____

_____

_____

_____

_____

_____

_____

Has talking to a therapist or counsellor been helpful? (Everyone may not have needed therapy) How has a spiritual accountability partner helped?

_____

_____

_____

_____

_____

_____

_____

_____

_____

_____

_____

_____

_____

_____

Did you feel inwardly cleansed when you submitted to baptism in the name of Jesus in accordance to Acts 2:38?

_____

_____

_____

_____

_____

_____

_____

_____

_____

_____

_____

_____

How does your new mindset and lifestyle of holiness balance out your decision making?

_____

_____

_____

_____

_____

_____

_____

_____

_____

_____

_____

_____

_____

Where do you consider yourself to be on the 30, 60, and 100-fold scale? Are you still struggling with a stronghold, or developing self- control/refraining from temptation, or have you outgrown and conquered the spirit that once had you bound?

_____

_____

_____

_____

_____

_____

_____

_____

_____

_____

_____

_____

Have you adapted to a lifestyle of prayer and fasting? (Matthew 17:21 This kind does not go out except prayer and fasting)

_____

_____

_____

_____

_____

_____

_____

_____

_____

_____

_____

_____

_____

_____

Your presentation, mannerisms, and thought patterns should be evolving if you commit to the process. Do you feel comfortable yet with your new identity?

_____

_____

_____

_____

_____

_____

_____

_____

_____

_____

_____

_____

_____

Taking one day at a time is important to minimize anxiety. Have you began to cast your cares on the Lord? (1 Peter 5:7).

_____

_____

_____

_____

_____

_____

_____

_____

_____

_____

_____

_____

Benefits of the Holy Spirit

Helps Us- Rom. 8:26

Guides Us- Jn. 16:13

Teaches Us- Jn. 14:26

Speaks- Rev. 2:7

Reveals- 1 Cor. 2:10

Instructs- Acts 829

Testifies of Jesus- Jn. 15:26

Comforts Us -Acts 9:31

Calls Us -Acts 13:2

Fills Us -Acts 4:31

He Strengthens Us- Eph. 3:16

Prays for Us- Rom. 8:26

Prophesies Through Us- 2 Pet. 1:21

Bears Witness to the Truth- Rom. 9:1

Brings Joy- 1 Thess. 1:6

Brings Freedom- 2 Cor. 3:17

Helps to Obey- 1 Pet. 1:22

Calls for Jesus' Return- Rev. 22:17

Transforms Us- 2 Cor. 3:18

Lives in Us- 1 Cor. 3:16

Frees Us- Rom. 8:2

Renews Us- Titus 3:5

Gives Gifts- 1 Cor. 12:8-10

Produces Fruit in Us- Gal. 5:22-23

Leads Us- Rom. 8:14

Convicts- Jn. 16:8

Sanctifies Us- 2 Thess. 2:13

Empowers Us- Acts 1:8

Unites Us- Eph. 4:3-4

Seals Us- Eph. 1:13

Gives Access to the Father- Eph. 2:18

Enables Us to Wait- Gal. 5:5

Casts Out Demons- Matt. 12:28